WOODWIND
INSTRUMENTS

by
John Wood

Minneapolis, Minnesota

Credits

All images are courtesy of Shutterstock.com, unless otherwise specified. With thanks to Getty Images, Thinkstock Photo, and iStockphoto. Recurring – paw, Visual Unit, Trikona. Cover – NotionPic, StockSmartStart, ac_yotto. Page 2–3 – stockphoto-graf. Page 4–5 – AngelaGrant. Page 6–7 – Boris Medvedev, Juanan Barros Moreno. Page 8–9 – Andrey_Popov, David Kabot, CC BY 2.0 <https://creativecommons.org/licenses/by/2.0>, via Wikimedia Commons. Page 10–11 – Boris Medvedev, ZUMA Press, Inc. Page 12–13 – Sönke Kraft aka Arnulf zu Linden, trigga, CC BY-SA 3.0 <http://creativecommons.org/licenses/by-sa/3.0/>, via Wikimedia Commons, Baishev. Page 14–15 – AGCuesta. Page 16–17 – Maljalen, Away. Page 18–19 – Dusyatko, Nomad_Soul. Page 20–21 – Hannes Wiedmann, CC BY-SA 4.0 <https://creativecommons.org/licenses/by-sa/4.0/>, via Wikimedia Commons, University of Edinburgh, CC BY 3.0 <https://creativecommons.org/licenses/by/3.0/>, via Wikimedia Commons, Lunja, Maria-Kitaeva. Page 22–23 – Jack.Q, Yusnizam Yusof, pxl.store, RnDmS.

Bearport Publishing Company Product Development Team

President: Jen Jenson; Director of Product Development: Spencer Brinker; Managing Editor: Allison Juda; Associate Editor: Naomi Reich; Associate Editor: Tiana Tran; Art Director: Colin O'Dea; Designer: Kim Jones; Designer: Kayla Eggert; Product Development Assistant: Owen Hamlin

Library of Congress Cataloging-in-Publication Data

Names: Wood, John, 1990- author.
Title: Woodwind instruments / by John Wood.
Description: Fusion books. | Minneapolis : Bearport Publishing Company, 2024. | Series: All about instruments | Includes index.
Identifiers: LCCN 2024007023 (print) | LCCN 2024007024 (ebook) | ISBN 9798889169697 (library binding) | ISBN 9798892324793 (paperback) | ISBN 9798892321150 (ebook)
Subjects: LCSH: Woodwind instruments--Juvenile literature.
Classification: LCC ML931 .W56 2024 (print) | LCC ML931 (ebook) | DDC 788.2/19--dc23/eng/20240116
LC record available at https://lccn.loc.gov/2024007023
LC ebook record available at https://lccn.loc.gov/2024007024

© 2025 BookLife Publishing
This edition is published by arrangement with BookLife Publishing.

North American adaptations © 2025 Bearport Publishing Company. All rights reserved. No part of this publication may be reproduced in whole or in part, stored in any retrieval system, or transmitted in any form or by any means, electronic, mechanical, photocopying, recording, or otherwise, without written permission from the publisher. Bearport Publishing is a division of Chrysalis Education Group.

For more information, write to Bearport Publishing, 5357 Penn Avenue South, Minneapolis, MN 55419.

CONTENTS

Join the Band...................4
Instruments from History..........6
Making Sound with Woodwinds.....8
Bassoon......................10
Recorder.....................11
Clarinet......................12
Flute........................14
Piccolo......................16
Mijwiz.......................17
Saxophone...................18
Ocarina.....................20
Bagpipes....................21
What Will You Play?............22
Glossary....................24
Index.......................24

JOIN THE BAND

Do you love music? Have you ever wanted to play an instrument? Let's join a band!

This book is about woodwind instruments. Today, these instruments are made of wood or metal. But humans have been playing these types of instruments for much longer than we have been making them with metal.

Musicians in a band often play different instruments.

Instruments from History

One of the oldest instruments ever found is a flute made from a bird's bone.

ABOUT 4,500 YEARS AGO

40,000 YEARS AGO

Lyres are some of the oldest string instruments.

Djembe drums have been played at different events for hundreds of years.

ABOUT 800 YEARS AGO

ABOUT 300 YEARS AGO

The serpent is an instrument that was popular in the 1700s.

MAKING SOUND WITH WOODWINDS

Woodwind instruments can make music in different ways. Some have **reeds**. When a musician blows into the instrument, the reed **vibrates** the air inside. You hear these vibrations as sounds.

A REED

Woodwinds have holes. Covering different combinations of holes makes different **pitches**.

Musicians play woodwind instruments without reeds by blowing air through or across a mouthpiece. This also makes the air inside vibrate.

MOUTHPIECE

BASSOON

A bassoon is a long woodwind instrument. It has two small reeds that are tied together. They are attached to the instrument with a long metal tube called the bocal.

BELL RING

BOCAL

BOOT

Bassoons make deep buzzing sounds.

RECORDER

A recorder is a small instrument that makes high-pitched sounds. Players blow into the mouthpiece and cover the holes with their fingers to create different **notes**.

Recorders are usually made out of wood or plastic.

FINGER HOLE

MOUTHPIECE

CLARINET

A clarinet has a single reed. All along the instrument are keys and finger holes. Pressing different groups of keys and holes makes different notes.

FINGER HOLES

BELL

Clarinets come in different sizes that make different pitches.

DOREEN KETCHENS

Doreen Ketchens started learning the clarinet to get out of a history test when she was young. Since then, she has become a very famous clarinet player.

Doreen Ketchens has **performed** for four U.S. presidents.

FLUTE

KEY

FOOT JOINT

The flute is a small instrument that makes high-pitched sounds. It is made of three pieces that are fitted together. To play it, musicians hold the instrument sideways and blow across a hole in the mouthpiece.

In the past, flutes were made of wood or bone. Today, they are usually made of metal.

MOUTHPIECE

GREG PATTILLO

Some people are beatbox flute players. These musicians make a drum-like beat with their voices and mouths while also playing the flute.

Greg Pattillo is a famous beatbox flute player. Millions of people have watched videos of him playing.

PICCOLO

The piccolo is a very small instrument that is similar to the flute. It is the highest-pitched woodwind instrument in an **orchestra**.

The body of a piccolo is usually wood. The keys are often made of metal.

MIJWIZ

The mijwiz (MIJH-wiz) is a folk instrument from the Middle East. It is made of two pipes tied together, with finger holes running along the tubes. Musicians can make different notes by covering different holes while blowing into the instrument.

This instrument is made of bamboo reeds.

PIPES

FINGER HOLE

SAXOPHONE

The saxophone is a single-reed instrument that is usually made out of brass. There are six different types of saxophones played today. Each one is a different size.

A saxophone is made of about 600 parts.

NECK

BELL

BOW

ADOLPHE SAX

Adolphe Sax invented the saxophone in the 1840s.

Adolphe Sax almost didn't live to invent the saxophone. As a child, he swallowed a needle, drank acid, and was hit in the head by a brick!

OCARINA

FINGER HOLE

TAIL

MOUTHPIECE

An ocarina is a small instrument that is usually made of clay, metal, or plastic. It comes in different sizes and shapes, and can have as many as **12** holes.

Ocarinas were first played in Central America more than 4,500 years ago.

BAGPIPES

To play the bagpipes, you blow into the blowpipe and squeeze the bag. This makes a sound. Then, you cover the holes on the chanter pipe to change the pitch.

BLOWPIPE

CHANTER

BAG

Drone pipes stick out from the top and make a humming sound.

WHAT WILL YOU PLAY?

Now you know all about woodwind instruments! Pick your instrument and join a band.

Classical music has bassoons, clarinets, and other woodwind instruments.

Saxophones are very common in jazz bands.

Klezmer is a type of Jewish folk music that uses clarinets.

Flutes and whistles can be played on their own or with other instruments in **traditional** Malaysian and Irish folk music.

It is time to start playing!

Glossary

musicians people who make or play music

notes musical sounds of a certain pitch that last for a length of time

orchestra a group of musicians who play classical music together

performed done something in front of people

pitches the high and low sounds instruments can make

reeds thin strips of material that vibrate to make sound in woodwind instruments

traditional something that has stayed the same for many years

vibrates moves back and forth very quickly

Index

bands 4–5, 22
Ketchens, Doreen 13
keys 12, 14, 16
metal 5, 14, 16, 20
mouthpiece 9, 11–12, 14–15, 20
notes 11–12, 21
Pattillo, Greg 15
plastic 11, 20
reeds 8–10, 12, 17–18, 21
Sax, Adolphe 19
wood 5, 11, 14, 16